REPTILES

Please visit our web site at: **www.garethstevens.com**
For a free color catalog describing Gareth Stevens Publishing's list of
high-quality books and multimedia programs, call **1-800-542-2595 (USA)**
or **1-800-387-3178 (Canada)**. Gareth Stevens Publishing's fax: **(414) 332-3567**.

Library of Congress Cataloging-in-Publication Data

Slither.
    Reptiles.
       p. cm. — (Discovery Channel school science: the plant and animal
kingdoms)
    Summary: Presents information about various types of reptiles, creatures
who have lived on earth for almost 300 million years, including their evolutionary
history, physical characteristics, behavior, habitat, life cycle, and more.
    ISBN 0-8368-3219-1 (lib. bdg.)
    1. Reptiles—Juvenile literature. [1. Reptiles.] I. Title. II. Series.
QL644.2.S58   2002
597.96—dc21   2002021167

This edition first published in 2002 by
Gareth Stevens Publishing
A World Almanac Education Group Company
330 West Olive Street, Suite 100
Milwaukee, WI 53212 USA

Writers: Lelia Mander, Lew Parker

Photographs: Cover, alligator, © Corel; p. 2, alligators (both), © Corel; p. 3, frilled
lizard, © Klaus Uhlenhut/Animals Animals; pp. 4-5, alligator (side view), © Corel;
eggs hatching and alligator female moving eggs (both), © Chris Johns/National
Geographic Image Collection; pp. 7-8, New Zealand, © Corel; tuatara, © Doug
Wechsler/Animals Animals; pp. 8-9, dinosaurs, © Corel; p. 11, © Corel (both);
p. 12, giant tortoise, © Ralph Reinhold; Galápagos, © Corel; p. 13, Charles Darwin,
© Corbis; p. 14, turtles (both), © Patti Murray/Animals
Animals; diamondback terrapin, S. R. Maglione © 1997 Photo
Researchers, Inc.; p. 16, © Corel (both); shovel-nosed snake,
© Corel; worm lizard, © K. H. Switak; tuatara, © Doug
Wechsler/Animals Animals; pp. 18-19, cottonmouth snake,
© Stan Osolinski 1992/FPG; p. 20, thorny devil lizard,
© Dani Jeske/Animals Animals; fringe-toed lizard; © Zig
Leszczynski/Animals Animals; p. 21, frilled lizard, © Klaus

This U.S. edition © 2002 by Gareth Stevens, Inc. First published in 1999 as
Slither: The Reptile Files by Discovery Enterprises, LLC, Bethesda, Maryland.
© 1999 by Discovery Communications, Inc.

Further resources for students and educators available at
www.discoveryschool.com

Designed by Bill SMITH STUDIO
Designers: Eric Hoffsten, Jay Jaffe, Brian Kobberger, Nick Stone,
  Sonia Gauba
Photo Editor: Justine Price
Art Buyer: Lillie Caporlingua
Gareth Stevens Editor: Alan Wachtel
Gareth Stevens Art Director: Tammy Gruenewald

Printed in the United States of America

1 2 3 4 5 6 7 8 9 06 05 04 03 02

Uhlenhut/Animals Animals; p. 22, rattlesnake fangs, © C. W. Schwartz/Animals
Animals; crocodile, © Corel; alligator snapping turtle, © George Grall/National
Geographic Image Collection; p. 23, python constricting rat, © Zig Leszczynski/
Animals Animals; chameleon, © Corel; p. 24, leatherback sea turtle, © Jany
Sauvanet/Photo Researchers, Inc.; anaconda, © M. Wendler/Okapia/Photo
Researchers, Inc.; Malaysian flying dragon, © Zig Leszczynski/Animals Animals;
p. 25, giant tortoise, © Zig Leszczynski/Animals Animals; pp. 26-27, © Corel (both);
pp. 28-29, tundra, © Corel; p. 30, © Corel.

Illustrations: p. 5, reptile egg, and p. 14, turtle shells,
Christoper Burke

Acknowledgments: Excerpts from THE COURAGE OF TURTLES,
by Edward Hoagland. Copyright © Edward Hoagland. Reprinted
by permission of Random House, Inc. All rights reserved.

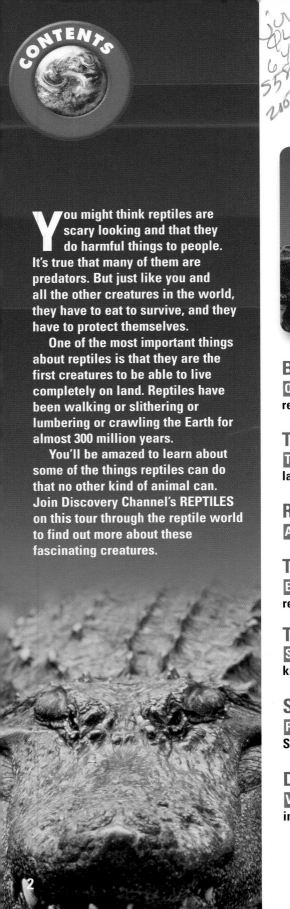

CONTENTS

You might think reptiles are scary looking and that they do harmful things to people. It's true that many of them are predators. But just like you and all the other creatures in the world, they have to eat to survive, and they have to protect themselves.

One of the most important things about reptiles is that they are the first creatures to be able to live completely on land. Reptiles have been walking or slithering or lumbering or crawling the Earth for almost 300 million years.

You'll be amazed to learn about some of the things reptiles can do that no other kind of animal can. Join Discovery Channel's REPTILES on this tour through the reptile world to find out more about these fascinating creatures.

REPTILES

Scare tactics... see page 21

Reptiles

Like fish, amphibians, birds, and you and your fellow mammals, reptiles are vertebrates, or animals with backbones. So how are reptiles different from other vertebrates? Reptiles don't require water to reproduce, as amphibians and fish do. Their bodies are covered with scales to keep them from drying out. Also, most reptiles give birth to their young on land. Some reptiles lay eggs, while a few produce live young from their bodies.

The main thing that separates reptiles from birds and mammals is that reptiles are exothermic. They can't regulate their own body temperature. This means their temperature is dictated by the temperature of the air around them. One way a lizard can get warm is to lie out in the sun and soak up the rays. Its body will then stay warm for a while, even after it moves into the shade. See for yourself what makes a reptile special. Features are characteristics that most reptiles share. Requirements are aspects that all reptiles have in common. Refer back to this page as much as you need to, or want to, as you read the book.

There are four different orders within the class Reptilia:

1. **Turtles and tortoises** [Testudines]
2. **Lizards and snakes** [Squamata]
3. **Crocodiles and alligators** [Crocodilia]
4. **Tuataras** [Rhynchocephalia]: the smallest order, but one that is 250 million years old. All tuataras live on islands off the coast of New Zealand.

(For more info, see the chart on pages 10-11, REPTILES ON PARADE)

REQUIREMENT: EXOTHERMIC—People call reptiles cold-blooded. But this doesn't mean that a reptile's blood is actually cold. Instead, exothermic means that a reptile can't regulate its own body temperature the way birds and mammals can. A reptile needs to rely on outside factors, such as the sun, to get warm. Amphibians and fish are also exothermic.

FEATURE: VERTEBRAE—All reptiles have a backbone, but not all vertebrate animals are reptiles. Many reptiles' vertebrae extend all the way to the tips of their powerful tails.

FEATURE: EYESIGHT—Many reptiles rely on their sharp eyesight to look out for prey. Chameleons' eyes can move independently of each other as they scan for insects. Crocodiles have specially adapted eyes for hunting at night.

REQUIREMENT: LUNGS—Without lungs, reptiles wouldn't be able to live on land. Lungs mean they can breathe without having to go back in the water or receive oxygen through their skin, as amphibians do.

FEATURE: SKIN—Having tough skin is key for any reptile's survival. Scales protect the reptile's body and also keep it from drying up. For this reason, some reptiles can survive in the desert. Scales are made of keratin, the same material that makes up your fingernails and hair.

REQUIREMENT: AMNIOTE—Without the special features of the amniote egg, there is no way reptiles would have made it onto land. Once fertilized, the reptile egg comes fully equipped to feed and protect the embryo until hatching time.

LEATHERY SHELL: Protects embryo and allows air in, but keeps vital fluids from leaking out

CHORION (KOR-EE ON): Tough membrane under the shell that surrounds all other membranes

ALLANTOIS (AH-LANT-TWAS): Stores wastes

YOLK SAC: Contains the embryo's food supply

AMNIOTIC SAC: Fluid-filled sac keeps embryo moist

EMBRYO: This baby alligator is about halfway through development.

FEATURE: REPRODUCTION—Some reptiles, such as certain species of snakes and lizards, give birth to live young. But most, including all species of turtles and crocodiles, lay eggs. As soon as they hatch, most reptile babies are on their own, although a mother alligator will help her young emerge from the nest and protect them from predators.

FEATURE: TEETH—Alligators and crocodiles use their teeth more for catching prey than for chewing. They will either swallow prey whole or tear it into smaller pieces before eating it. Some poisonous snakes have fangs, which they use to inject venom into their prey. But not all reptiles have teeth. Turtles have sharp edges on their jaws that they use to chop off plants or seaweed for food.

Activity

TAKING TEMPERATURE What is it like to be exothermic? Because you are a mammal, you are endothermic. Not only can you generate your own heat (measuring 98.6° F [37° C]), but you can pass this heat onto other things. A reptile, on the other hand, gets heat from the outside.

Try a few things to see the difference. First, sit on a chair for five minutes. Afterwards, stand up and feel the chair. Is it warmer than when you first sat down on it? Next, take two round objects, like rocks or rubber balls. Place one in the sun and one in the shade. After five minutes, pick them up, one in each hand, and compare their temperatures. Which one is warmer? Write down your observations. If the objects can represent reptiles, what conclusions can you draw about how reptiles react to temperatures, and how is this different from what you can do?

5

Bringing Up Baby

A Remote Island off the coast of New Zealand, Anytime

Q: You're kind of cute, for a lizard.

A: I'm not a lizard. I'm a tuatara.

Q: A what-ara?

A: A tuatara. I'm one of those reptiles that live only on a group of islands off the coast of New Zealand.

Q: You could've fooled me. You look like a lizard. And why don't you live anywhere else? I thought lizards lived all over the place.

A: But I'm a tuatara, not a lizard. And these islands are the only places in the world where I'm safe.

Q: Why's that?

A: Because so far these islands don't have any rats living on them. I'm scared to death of rats. So are my brothers and sisters.

Q: I am, too, but I can live with them. Can't you?

A: No. Rats eat small reptiles like me. They also eat reptile eggs. In fact, they ate so many tuatara babies and eggs that tuataras almost became extinct. If New Zealand hadn't split off from the mainland long before rats evolved here, we'd all be gone. As it is, we're endangered. There are only a few thousand of us. We used to live in New Zealand, but now we live only on the islands off the coast of New Zealand.

Q: So why don't you live on the mainland anymore?

A: Because in the early 19th century, Europeans came to New Zealand. They brought rats in their ships, which killed us off.

Q: But what about your parents? Wouldn't they protect you from rats?

A: Are you kidding? I'm not a lizard, but I *am* a reptile, in case you forgot.

Q: What difference should that make?

A: Well, reptile mothers don't generally stick around after they lay their eggs. We get deposited in a nest, often a shallow hole dug in the ground or between some rocks, and are left to fend for ourselves until we hatch. I'm only a week old, you know.

Q: So how did you survive?

A: Luckily, I get all the food I need right from inside my egg. The nutrition goes from the yolk sac straight to my stomach through the umbilical stalk. The egg has a leathery outer shell, which keeps all the fluids from drying up. Good thing, too, because, like all reptiles, I take a long time to hatch.

Q: How long?
A: More than a year. Fifteen months to be exact. That's the longest incubation period for any reptile.

Q: After all that time, how do you get out of the egg?
A: See this spike on the end of my nose? That's a special feature I have that's designed to help me break through the egg. Now that I'm out, I won't need it anymore. In a week or two, it'll fall off.

Q: You still haven't told me how you survive without your mother looking after you.
A: Unlike mammals, reptiles don't need a mother's milk. I can survive on the average adult tuatara diet— spiders, beetles, crickets.

Q: Gross! How can you stand it?
A: Simple—it's a matter of survival. Most reptiles eat animals of one kind or another. We're born fully developed, looking just like our parents, only smaller, and

ready to hunt for a living. Why, if I were a baby poisonous snake, I'd be fully equipped with deadly venom from the get-go. But I do get some help with my hunting.

Q: Who helps you?
A: The birds. Tuataras have a special relationship to the birds. Sea birds such as terns, petrels, and cormorants leave their droppings on the soil and rocks, which attract insects. We come out at night to feast. Sometimes we actually share burrows with petrels. We sleep in the burrow during the day, when the birds are out diving for fish, and then we go out when they come back. In the winters, the birds migrate, and we use the burrows for hibernation.

Q: I didn't know reptiles could hibernate. How do you do that?
A: We have what's called a low metabolic rate, meaning that we can survive without using much energy. Also, we've had millions of years to adapt to the cooler climate here. At temperatures of six degrees Celsius, our pulse can go as slow as ten heartbeats per minute, and we take only one breath per hour. This means we don't need a lot of food for energy when it's cold out. Occasionally, when the sun is out

during the day, we like to bask on the rocks and let the sun's heat warm us up on the inside. We feel safe on these islands.

Q: But what about your enemies, the rats?
A: Fortunately, people now understand that we're endangered, and they've passed laws to protect us. People aren't allowed to land on these islands, and that means rats aren't likely to land here, either. Anyway, most of the islands are surrounded by sheer cliffs that drop sharply into the sea. Not a good place to land a ship. So, we're protected by our habitat, but also by conservationists.

Q: How many of you are left?
A: Only about 10,000, and we're not a fast-growing population, either.

Q: How come?
A: Because it takes so long to reproduce. I won't be old enough to mate for another 20 years. Once they've been fertilized by the males, females can carry eggs around for as long as a year before laying them.

Q: Well, I guess you'd better be careful, so you'll live long enough to have babies of your own. Happy hunting!

Activity

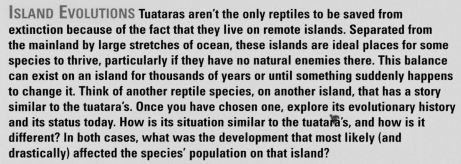

ISLAND EVOLUTIONS Tuataras aren't the only reptiles to be saved from extinction because of the fact that they live on remote islands. Separated from the mainland by large stretches of ocean, these islands are ideal places for some species to thrive, particularly if they have no natural enemies there. This balance can exist on an island for thousands of years or until something suddenly happens to change it. Think of another reptile species, on another island, that has a story similar to the tuatara's. Once you have chosen one, explore its evolutionary history and its status today. How is its situation similar to the tuatara's, and how is it different? In both cases, what was the development that most likely (and drastically) affected the species' population on that island?

THE GOLDEN AGE

To find out about the first reptiles, we need to travel way, way back in time—almost 300 million years. According to fossil discoveries, that's when the first reptiles appeared on Earth. Over millions of years, reptiles changed dramatically to adapt to alterations in Earth's climate and landscape. You won't believe some of the old "dinosaurs" we'll meet!

← PALEOZOIC ERA →

CARBONIFEROUS PERIOD (Pennsylvanian)
350–286 million years ago

PERMIAN PERIOD
286–248 million years ago

TRIASSIC PERIOD
248–208 million years ago

Reptiles evolve from amphibians

Amphibians, which can live on land and in water, rule. But amphibians have to lay their eggs in water. Then, some start laying their eggs on dry land. Soon these creatures can live on land, too. These are the first reptiles.

Reptiles of all kinds

Reptiles are everywhere. There are many varieties, each with special adaptations to help them thrive on land. Dimetrodon, for example, has a sail-like feature standing up on its back that may help it absorb heat from the Sun. Another reptile, Diadectes, is one of the first land animals to eat plants. Yum!

Dinosaurs make their entrance

Unlike other reptiles, such as lizards and crocodiles, whose legs are bent at an angle, dinosaurs have straight legs. Ancestors of turtles and crocodiles appear. Some Triassic dinosaurs, like Nothosaurus, live in the ocean. One of the first dinosaurs ever is Coelophysis. Believe it or not, this dinosaur is thought to have been a cannibal.

OF REPTILES

JURASSIC PERIOD
208–144 million years ago

CRETACEOUS PERIOD
144–65 million years ago

65 million years ago

Enormous dinosaurs everywhere!

By now, there are many different kinds of plant-eating dinosaurs. Some of these are huge, like Stegosaurus and Diplodocus, which are as long as 88 feet (27 m)! Some reptiles, including Pterosaurus, can fly, and others, like Elasmosaurus and Ichthyosaurus, swim in the sea. Elasmosaurus is 50 feet (15 m) long and has a neck the size of a giraffe's. Ichthyosaurus is more fishlike, using fins to steer.

Dinosaurs' heyday

More than half of the dinosaurs we know about thrive during this period. These include the huge and ferocious meat eater Tyrannosaurus and large-skulled Torosaurus. But some dinosaurs of this period are amazingly small, such as Compsognathus, which is only 28 inches (70 cm) long.

Glory days come to an end

All of a sudden, most dinosaurs become extinct. Some scientists think a meteor struck Earth. The explosion would have sent so much dust and debris into the atmosphere that the Sun's light was blocked for a long period, perhaps as much as six months. This caused a great many plants to die, and so the mighty dinosaurs, many of which lived on plants, couldn't survive. Nor could the dinosaurs that lived on plant-eating dinosaurs.

Activity

SURVIVAL GEAR Dinosaurs adapted to many different ways of life. Some were herbivores, or plant eaters, and others were carnivores, or meat eaters. Visit the dinosaur hall of a natural history museum or look at an illustrated book about dinosaurs, and compare these two different categories. Put your notes into a chart, with two vertical columns, one for herbivores and the other for carnivores. To the left side, list these features:
► overall size
► length of neck
► features in feet and legs
► teeth and jaws
► horns
Fill in descriptive notes for each feature in the two columns. How do these two types of dinosaurs differ?

REPTILES ON PARADE

Scientists divide the class Reptilia into four different orders. They all have important features in common, making them all reptiles, but they have key differences as well. These mainly have to do with outer appearance, but there are also distinctive internal differences.

ORDER		COMMON NAME	NO. OF SPECIES	WHERE IN THE WORLD
Testudines		Turtles and Tortoises	260	Temperate and tropical regions around the world
Squamata	SUBORDER Sauria	Lizards	4,000+	North and South America, Europe (south of Norway), Asia, Africa, islands in Atlantic, Pacific, and Indian oceans
	SUBORDER Serpentes	Snakes	2,600+	Temperate and tropical regions on all continents except Antarctica; not found on some islands, including Iceland and New Zealand
Crocodilia		Crocodiles	22	Tropical and subtropical regions of Africa, Latin America, Asia, and United States
Rhynchocephalia		Tuataras	2	Islands off New Zealand coast

ENDANGERED REPTILES: UNITED STATES

REPTILE	LOCATION
Alabama red-bellied turtle	Alabama
American crocodile	Florida
Blunt-nosed leopard lizard	Virgin Islands
Culebra Island giant anole	Puerto Rico and Culebra Island
Green sea turtle	Florida (uses coastal areas for breeding)
Kemp's ridley sea turtle	Padre Island, Florida (breeding ground)
Leatherback sea turtle	U.S. coastal waters
Mona ground iguana	Mona Island, Puerto Rico
Monito gecko	Puerto Rico
Plymouth red-bellied turtle	Massachusetts
Puerto Rican boa	Puerto Rico
San Francisco garter snake	San Francisco
Virgin Islands tree boa	Virgin Islands

Some Venomous Reptiles

SNAKES		LIZARDS
cobra	mamba	Gila monster
copperhead	rattlesnake	Mexican
coral snake	sea snake	beaded
cottonmouth	taipan	lizard
krait	viper	

HABITAT	EXAMPLES	CHARACTERISTICS
Salt water, fresh water, forests, arid and semiarid regions	Musk turtle, terrapin turtle, snapping turtle, land tortoise, sea turtle	Bony shell, rounded on back with flat belly, covering most of body; no teeth but sharp jaws for cutting; egg layer; plant eater
Tropical and temperate forests, mountains, deserts, grasslands	Gecko, Komodo dragon, chameleon, iguana, monitor lizard, legless lizard	Lots of varieties: many different colors and sizes; most are 4-legged with tail; most lay eggs, but some species give birth to live young; most have ear openings and eyelids
Tropical and temperate forests, mountains, desert and semiarid regions, oceans	Rattlesnake, anaconda, European adder, boa constrictor, coral snake, water moccasin	Long, slender bodies with no legs; move by pushing body from side to side; broad scales on belly to help forward movement; all are meat eaters; some have venom in fangs; flicking, forked tongues; no eyelids or ear openings
Freshwater and saltwater streams, rivers, lakes, swamps, and other wetlands	American alligator, Nile crocodile, caiman, gharial	Sharp eyesight with night vision; large size, ranging from 5 to 27 feet (1–8 m) long; large and powerful tail for swimming; big snout; throat flap to keep water out of windpipe; swim with eyes and nostrils above water; 4-chambered heart, unlike other reptiles, whose hearts all have only 3 chambers
Coastal forest or scrub, rocky areas	Tuatara	Row of spines along backbone and back of neck; remnant of third eye on head serves to recognize shades of dark and light and help regulate release of hormones

Desert Dwellers

SNAKES	LIZARDS
California glossy snake	chuckwalla
shovel-nosed snake	desert iguana
sidewinder	fringe-toed sand lizard
western diamondback rattlesnake	Gila monster
western patch-nosed snake	horned lizard
	leopard lizard
TURTLES	spiny lizard
gopher tortoise	thorny devil
saddleback tortoise	

Activity

WARMING TREND Look up the terms "temperate" and "tropical" in a dictionary and write down the definitions as they apply to places on Earth. Why are these words so important in describing where reptiles live? Based on what you know about reptiles, list two or three reasons why there are no reptiles in Antarctica.

The Giant Tortoise

Giant tortoises roamed much of the world half a million years ago, and then they almost died out completely. Today, the only surviving giant tortoises live in the Seychelles and in the Galápagos Archipelago. Located about 600 miles (965 km) from the west coast of South America, the Galápagos consist of 15 large islands and dozens of smaller ones. Some of these islands, created from volcanoes under the surface of the Pacific Ocean, are over four million years old.

The Galápagos are home to many rare creatures. Some of these species became extinct everywhere else in the world but survived on the Galápagos. On this small network of islands, they were safe from the predators who had killed them off elsewhere on the planet. The giant tortoises are just one group of these miraculous survivors.

In 1832, Charles Darwin set out on a voyage around the world. As a passenger aboard the *H.M.S. Beagle,* Darwin recorded his observations in his notebooks. The *Beagle* reached the Galápagos Islands three years later, and Darwin remained there for five weeks.

In these excerpts from his journal, Darwin describes the remarkable giant tortoises.

These animals ... grow to immense size: Mr. Lawson, an Englishman and vice-governor of the colony, told us that he had seen several so large, that it required six or eight men to lift them from the ground; and that some had afforded as much as two hundred pounds of meat. The old males are the largest, the females rarely growing to so great a size; the male can readily be distinguished from the female by the greater length of its tail. The tortoises which live on those islands where there is no water ... feed chiefly on the succulent cactus. Those which frequent the higher and damp regions, eat the leaves of various trees, a kind of berry which is acid, and likewise a pale green lichen, that hangs from the boughs of the trees.

The tortoise is very fond of water, drinking large quantities, and wallowing in the mud. The larger islands alone possess springs, and these are always situated towards the central parks, and at a considerable height. The tortoises, therefore, when thirsty, are obliged to travel from a long distance. Hence broad and well-beaten paths branch off in every direction from the wells down to the seacoast. When the tortoise arrives in the spring, he buries his head in the water above his eyes, and greedily swallows great mouthfuls, at the rate of about ten in a minute. The inhabitants say each animal stays

and the *H.M.S. Beagle*

PACIFIC OCEAN

SOUTH AMERICA

Galápagos Islands

three or four days in the neighborhood of the water, and then returns to the lower country.

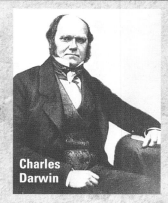

Charles Darwin

They travel a distance of about eight miles in two or three days. One large tortoise ... walked at the rate of sixty yards in ten minutes, that is 360 yards in the hour, or four miles a day—allowing a little time for it to eat on the road.

During the breeding season, when the male and female are together, the male utters a hoarse roar or bellowing, which, it is said, can be heard at the distance of more than a hundred yards. The female never uses her voice, and the male only at these times. They were at this time (October) laying their eggs. The female, where the soil is sandy, deposits them together, and covers them up with sand; but where the ground is rocky she drops them in any hole. The egg is white and spherical; one which I measured was seven inches and three-eighths in circumference. The young tortoises, as soon as they are hatched, fall prey in great numbers to buzzards. The old ones seem generally to die from accidents, as from falling down precipices.

The inhabitants believe that these animals are absolutely deaf; certainly they do not overhear a person walking close behind them.

South America, early 1900s

Not all reptile watchers were as peacefully observant as Darwin. Some fired their weapons first and asked questions later. Colonel Percy Fawcett, a British army officer, describes what happened on a trip down the Rio Negro:

"We were drifting easily along the sluggish current ... when almost under the bow there appeared a triangular head and several feet of undulating body. It was a giant anaconda. I sprang for my rifle as the creature began to make its way up the bank, and hardly waiting to aim smashed a .44 soft-nosed bullet into its spine, ten feet below the wicked head. At once there was a flurry of foam, and several heavy thumps along the boat's keel, shaking us as though we had run on a snag."

Activity

REPTILE RECORDS Darwin was a scientist who kept good notes during his travels. Pretend you're one of Darwin's colleagues and find a reptile to observe and write about. Perhaps your school has a terrarium with a lizard or small snake in it. If not, spend an afternoon at your local zoo. Choose one animal to watch, and jot down your observations in a notebook. How does the animal move? What does it look like? Describe its shape, size, and color. Pay especially close attention to its behavior when eating and interacting with other animals. Then, flesh out your notes into complete sentences and write a detailed portrait for Darwin to read.

Take it Slow

There are more than 260 species of turtles in the world today. Some are amphibious, meaning that they live both on land and in water. Some live in salt water, others in fresh water. Some live entirely on land. Turtles come in all different sizes. They belong to the order Testudines, which has been around for more than 200 million years. The largest turtle that ever lived was *Archelon,* which is now extinct. This giant sea turtle was as long as 11 feet (3.3 m)! Its shell would be big enough to use as a table to feed a family of four.

You can tell a turtle by its shell

Speaking of shells, what all turtles and tortoises have in common is the large shell on their backs. This is part of a turtle's skeleton. The curved upper part, the carapace, is supported by the backbone. The lower part, or the plastron, protects the turtle's belly. Most turtles' shells are made of a hard bony material that is covered by a top layer of keratin. Did you know you have keratin, too? Take a look at the outer layer of your fingernails and toenails. Same stuff.

The shape of a turtle's shell gives you clues about how and where the turtle lives.

High dome
This shell belongs to a heavy and slow-going land tortoise.

Slightly flattened
Turtles with this kind of shell live both on land and in water.

Flattened
This shell shape allows pond turtles to dive to the bottom of ponds.

Streamlined
The finlike ridges at the shell's edge and the way the plates are arranged help keep a swimming sea turtle on course.

Neckwise
Turtles are divided into two different groups, depending on how they tuck their heads under their shells. Hidden-necked turtles can bend their necks in a vertical S-shaped curve and hide their heads completely. Side-necked turtles have longer necks and flatter shells. They turn their heads to one side and tuck it under the shell. Side-necked turtles live in tropical areas of Africa, Australia, and South America.

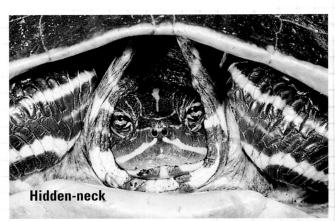

Hidden-neck

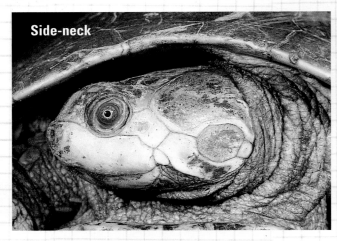

Side-neck

Turtle or Tortoise?

All tortoises are turtles, but not all turtles are tortoises. You know it's a tortoise if it

- lives in deserts and arid regions;
- eats only plants;
- has a large, hard, domelike shell;
- is hidden-necked;
- moves slowly: 295 ft (90 m) per hour.

Odd one out: The African pancake tortoise has a flat shell that is soft, allowing it to squeeze between rocks.

Turtles in Indian myth and legend

According to the Muskegee Creek Indians, the first animal was a turtle named Locv. The world was covered completely with water. Locv taught all other animals how to swim and then made land out of huge piles of mud. Some peoples believed a turtle carried the whole world on its back. The Iroquois named one of their clans after the turtle and used a turtle symbol on the door of their meeting house.

Fun facts
about turtles

- ► been around for 200 million years
- ► can't leave their shells
- ► live long lives—Some live up to 100 years, but you can't tell a turtle's age by the "growth rings" found on some turtles' shells.

Activity

HOME TOWN Sea turtles swim for thousands of miles, covering a large area as they search for food. But when it's time to breed, most species return to the same beach where they were born, no matter how far away. Imagine if this were the pattern for human beings and think about your own family. Make a chart, listing your grandparents and then your parents. How far would each person have to travel in order to have children? Using an atlas, measure the distance between each person's home today and his or her birthplace. Figure out which side of your family would have traveled the greatest number of miles by the time you were born.

Similar... but Different

Although scientists divide reptiles into different orders, suborders, families, and species, some reptiles look an awful lot alike. How can we tell the difference between, say, a legless lizard and a snake? How about a crocodile and an alligator? See if these pictures shed any light on a sometimes dim and confusing situation.

How do you tell an alligator from a crocodile?

- Alligators have wide heads, and their noses are rounded in a U shape. Crocodile heads are narrower, and their snouts end in a sharper, V-shaped point.

- Both have a large tooth on the lower jaw, but a crocodile's tooth fits into a notch in the upper jaw and still shows when the mouth is closed. In alligators, this tooth fits into a pit in the upper jaw and is hidden when the mouth is closed.

- Crocodiles are more aggressive than alligators, which are more likely to slip away rather than confront danger head-on.

American alligator
Alligator mississipiensis

African long-snouted crocodile

Crocodylis cataphractus

Lizard without legs – or snake?

We think of lizards as reptiles with legs. All reptiles with no legs are snakes, right? Well, not necessarily. The lizard family includes the worm lizards, 140 species of lizards that live underground. All but three of these have no legs. Because they spend their lives burrowing through soil, feeding on ants and other insects, worm lizards don't need legs. The typical worm lizard uses its specially shaped head to move loose soil out of the way.

Although it's long and slender and has no legs, you know a worm lizard isn't a small snake because:

1 All snakes have forked tongues, while worm lizards' tongues end in a point.

2 Worm lizards have tiny ear openings behind their eyes, while snakes have no ear openings at all.

Worm lizard
Rhineuvra

Shovel-nosed snake
Chionactis occipitalis

When is a lizard look-alike not a lizard?

New Zealand, 80 million years ago

When it's a tuatara! Tuataras look a lot like lizards, particularly the larger species, such as horned or dragon lizards, but they differ in important ways. Tuataras have a row of sharp, bony spines along their necks and backs, which makes them look like holdovers from the dinosaur days. Once, these spikes probably protected tuataras from other reptile enemies. The official name of the tuatara group is Rhynchocephalia, which means "beak head."

The tuatara order has been around for 240 million years. Tuataras have geography and geology to thank for their miraculous survival. Like a lot of dinosaurs, they were almost completely wiped out by mammals that ate their eggs and young. But about 80 million years ago, before mammals evolved, New Zealand drifted apart from other major land masses. A lone community of tuataras survived, safe from these predators. Today, the only remaining tuataras live on about 30 small islands off the coast of New Zealand.

Tuatara
Sphenodon punctatus

DOING THE SNAKE DANCE

You know a snake when you see one. For one thing, all snakes are completely covered with overlapping scales. Larger scales protect the snake's belly. Arranged horizontally, these give the snake traction as it moves along the ground or up a tree. You'll see different kinds of colors and patterns on a snake's skin, depending on where it lives. Some snakes are brightly colored, which is a warning to other animals that they might be poisonous. Others are camouflaged so that they blend in perfectly with their surroundings. All snakes shed the outer layer of skin as they grow bigger, a process called molting.

But what is it like inside a snake? What if you could become very, very small and take a round-trip journey— safely—through a snake's body? Come on in and see for yourself. The snake we are going to visit is frozen in time. It lies completely still, with its mouth wide open. You are traveling inside a special "snake voyager pod," which is no bigger than a grain of rice.

This snake's mouth is wide open—so wide, in fact, that our vessel can go in without touching any of its teeth or its tongue. Snakes have a special kind of jaw that allows them to swallow their prey in one piece, even if the animal is bigger than they are. It's like being double-jointed. The lower jaw and the head are connected by elastic muscle tissue, so that, when the snake wants to swallow an animal or a large egg, its lower jaw opens wide both at the front and the back of its mouth, and also from side to side.

Up above you are the snake's two fangs. Don't mess with these! Ordinarily, they lie flat against the roof of the snake's mouth. But because this snake was frozen just at the moment it opened its mouth wide, the fangs are out and ready for action. The second these sharp teeth sink into another animal's flesh, they release poison, or venom, from a nearby gland.

Down below is the snake's forked tongue. Snakes flick their tongues when aroused. Believe it or not, this is how they "smell" what's in the air around them. The tongue picks up microscopic particles and transmits information to a special organ, called the Jacobson's organ, in the snake's head. This feature helps a snake track down its prey.

Feel a little dizzy? This is because the snake is all coiled up and you're going around and around and around. Snakes assume this position for several different reasons. A mother might coil herself around her eggs to protect them or keep them warm. A snake such as a boa constrictor may wrap itself around an animal as a way to suffocate it slowly; every time the animal takes in a breath, the snake squeezes just a little harder, until the animal can't breathe anymore and dies. A coiled-up snake is also a scary sight to potential predators. For some nonpoisonous snakes, coiling is their only defense. Most snakes, however, coil for warmth.

Because snakes are so long and thin, their organs are shaped and arranged differently than ours. This snake, for example, only has one lung; its left lung disappeared long ago. Check out how long and thin this lung is! Not to mention its liver. And this snake's kidneys are in a line, one in front of the other. Humans have one kidney on either side.

Steer your voyager pod to get a closer look. The row of curved vertical bones are the snake's ribs. You'll see that they are all attached at the top to the snake's backbone. Although its body is shaped a bit like a worm's, the snake can't be a worm because it has a backbone. The ribs are connected to each other by muscle. Lacking feet or legs, snakes use this muscle to move themselves from place to place. They might push sideways and move forward, somewhat like a fish, or they might stiffen themselves and stretch forward, as a tree snake does when it goes from one branch to another.

At last, your journey has reached its end, the tip of the snake's tail. Most snakes' tails come to a pointed tip, but the rattlesnake's tail ends in a series of hollow interconnected chambers. A new chamber is added each time a rattlesnake sheds its skin. The rattlesnake makes a distinctive and scary buzzing noise with its tail by tensing its muscles and shaking the tail. This tail, although frozen, is standing straight up. Let's turn our snake voyager pod around and zoom right out of here, just in case the snake decides it's time to wake up. We'll go right back the way we came, as quickly as possible. Are you holding on tight? Then, let's go. See ya, snake, it's been real!

Activity

PREDATOR IN ACTION Imagine the virtual snake "comes to life" as soon as your voyager pod shoots out of its mouth. Remember the position the snake was in; based on what you've learned, what do you suppose the snake was about to do? Now, imagine that a small mammal, such as a gopher or rat, is nearby, and describe, step by step, what happens next. What gives you the feeling the small mammal doesn't wind up as safely as you did?

The Best Defense is a Weird Offense

Some reptiles, such as crocodiles and venomous snakes, are notorious predators. But did you know that most reptiles are also prey? Other animals, including birds and small mammals, go after reptiles' eggs and young. And reptiles have certainly been known to go after other reptiles, as well. Lizards, in particular, have to worry because their small size makes them appealing as food for birds, snakes, and carnivorous mammals. To protect themselves from danger, lizards have devised some unusual defenses.

Armed (and dangerous?)

Some lizards, such as the thorny devil, have prickly "horns" protruding from their skin. These small bones are called osteoderms, meaning "bony skin." FYI, the ridges on the back of an alligator are also osteoderms. This hard, bony layer protects the lizard's body from being pierced or stabbed by an enemy. A predator sees an armored lizard and decides it's way too much trouble to eat.

Run for your life! The first line of defense is evasive action. Move quickly, find a safe place to hide. Some lizards can run very fast using bipedal locomotion, which means using just their hind legs. The basilisk has perfected bipedal locomotion to an artform. This iguana from Central America has special fringes on its long rear toes (shown above) that allow it to run over water. It uses its long tail as a counterbalance. As the basilisk slows down, it drops into the water and swims away.

Camouflage Most lizards will try to blend in with their natural surroundings. A dappled brown and purple gecko is just the right color for its rocky desert environment, while a green iguana looks just like the tree branch it's sleeping on. The chameleon is the best faker of all; it can change its colors to suit its surroundings, choosing from shades of green, yellow, brown, and gray. Chameleons have special skin cells, called chromatophores, that contain different pigments. These pigments can move closer to or farther away from the skin, depending on what color the chameleon's nervous system says would offer the best disguise. The pigment closest to the skin determines the skin's color.

Tails of all types One way to escape a predator is to distract it. The zebra-tailed lizard, when facing one of its foes, will wave its snazzy, black-and-white tail to make the attacker focus on a nonvital part of its body or to show that it is aware of the attacker. The lizard, which is very fast, can then run away, leaving the attacker in a trance and completely stopped in its tracks.

Tail-dropping is another escape technique, although a drastic one. Skinks and geckos have long, slender tails. When a predator grabs the lizard, it contracts its tail muscles. This causes an area along the tail vertebrae to fracture, so that the lizard's tail actually drops off. The attacker sees the still-wriggling tail on the ground, lets go of the lizard, and grabs the tail instead. The lizard runs away and grows a new tail over the next few months. On the downside, the new tail is not quite as strong as the original one. And this escape method can only be used once in a lizard's life.

Some really weird defenses

Scare tactics work, too. The Australian frilled lizard (shown below) will open its mouth wide, which causes a large frill of skin on either side of its neck to spread out like a fan. If that weren't scary enough, the lizard also lashes its tail back and forth and makes loud, hissing sounds.

The African armadillo lizard has spines all over its body. When threatened, it curls up into a ball and covers its belly with its fence-like, prickly tail.

Some enemies can't stand the sight of blood. The horned lizard will squirt its own blood from tiny vessels near its eyes to scare off its attacker. It can shoot a stream of blood out three feet (1 m).

WILL HUNT FOR FOOD

Most reptiles eat meat in the form of fish, small mammals, birds, insects, or other reptiles. Here are some species that have developed ingenious ways to pursue and kill their prey in the fastest and most efficient ways possible.

Pick your POISON

Some snakes use venom to subdue and kill their victims. This poison gives them an edge, since they don't have arms or claws to grab their prey. A snake can bite a small mammal and then follow its trail to the spot where the animal collapses. There are two types of venom, both deadly. One paralyzes, the other starts destroying the victim's muscle tissue, which gives the snake a head start on digesting its meal.

GONE FISHIN'

Turtles that live in the water feed on small fish, mollusks, and water bugs. Some turtles have ingenious ways of hunting for fish. The alligator snapping turtle, for example, has a built-in lure in its mouth, a pink, squiggly thing that looks like a worm. The alligator snapping turtle sits at the bottom of the pond, opens its mouth, and waves its tongue. Thinking it's found a worm, a fish swims closer. Snap go the alligator turtle's mighty jaws.

The matamata also lurks at the bottom, in disguise. It moves little flaps on its ears and head that look like interesting and tasty tidbits to passing fish. The matamata suddenly opens its huge, v-shaped mouth, creating a vacuum that sucks the fish inside, along with a big gulp of water.

Looks like a log to me!

Crocodilian hunters rely on the element of surprise. They lurk just underwater, completely still and in disguise. Only their eyes and nostrils are above the surface. They use their excellent eyesight to scan for prey at the water's edge. Once an alligator sees something, a water bird for instance, it can swim over and have the prey in its jaws in a matter of seconds.

THE BIG SQUEEZE

All snakes have to eat, but not all snakes are poisonous. Those that aren't have to kill another way. They lie in wait and attack their prey off guard. Then, they wrap themselves around the animal, squeezing tighter and tighter until the animal's blood can't circulate and it can't breathe. The snake then opens its mouth wide and slowly swallows the dead animal whole.

TONGUE-TWISTER

The chameleon is a lizard with a very long tongue that is sticky on the end. It hunts insects and captures them by shooting out its tongue, trapping them on the sticky end. For stability, the chameleon wraps its tail and hind feet around the branch where it lies in wait for unsuspecting bugs nearby.

South Africa, mid-20th Century

What do you do if you meet a python that wants to eat you? Here is some highly questionable advice from a writer advising missionaries working in South Africa:

Remember not to run away, the python can move faster. Lie flat on the ground on your back with your feet together, arms to the side ... The python will then try to push its head under you ... Keep calm, one wiggle and he will get under you, wrap his coils around you and crush you to death. After a time the python will get tired of this and will probably decide to swallow you ... He will very likely begin with one of your feet. Keep calm. You must let him swallow your foot. It is quite painless and will take a long time ... Wait patiently until he has swallowed up to your knee. Then carefully take out your knife and insert it into the distended side of his mouth and with a quick rip slit him up.

REPTILE HALL

Living Large

The world's largest lizard is the adult male Komodo dragon, found in Indonesia. The largest one ever recorded was 10 feet 2 inches (3 m) long and 365 pounds (166 kg)! The Komodo can eat animals as large as goats—it simply swallows them whole. The largest snake is the anaconda, which can grow up to 30 feet long (10.9 m) and weigh as much as 550 pounds (250 kg). Meanwhile, the average ocean-dwelling leatherback turtle grows to 5 feet (1.5 m) long and weighs 800 pounds (365 kg), making it the world's heaviest reptile. Amazingly, the biggest leatherback ever found was 1,400 pounds (636 kg).

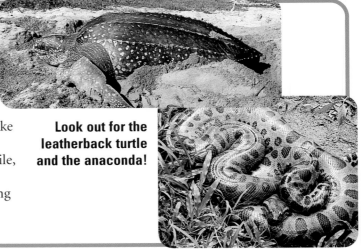

Look out for the leatherback turtle and the anaconda!

Largest poisonous snake

The king cobra, a carnivorous reptile found in southern Asia, often reaches a length of 18 feet (5.5 m). Its venom paralyzes the victim's nervous system. The king cobra has a neck hood that spreads to make the snake look larger to both enemies and prospective mates.

Smallest reptile

The world's smallest lizard is the rare Virgin Islands gecko. Geckos measure 0.70 inches (2 cm) from snout to vent, or nose to rear end. Only 15 of these tiny creatures have ever been found.

Flying reptiles

Ever seen a flying lizard? Some draco lizards have well-developed flaps on the skin attached to their rib cages. With these flaps, they can drop down great distances to escape a predator and glide down for a safe landing. Some snakes can glide, too: the flying tree snake launches itself from a tree branch and moves through the air in a straight line. Its curved belly works as a kind of parachute, helping to break the snake's fall to the ground (or a lower branch).

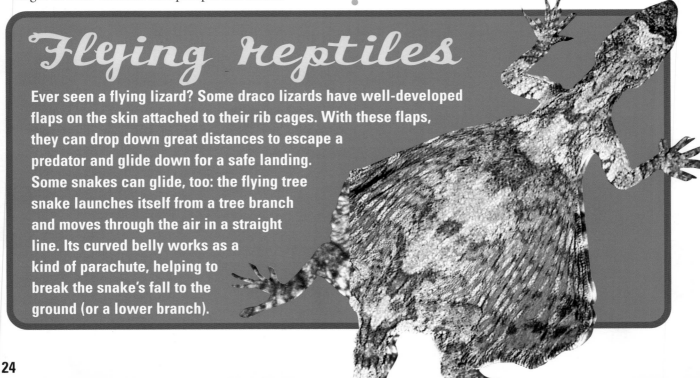

OF FAME

The tortoise and the lizard

It's no surprise that the slowest reptile is a turtle—and a big one, at that. Giant tortoises, found mainly in the Galápagos Islands, weigh up to 595 pounds (270 kg), which explains their sluggish pace. The world's fastest land reptile is the spiny-tailed iguana of Costa Rica. The 24-to-36-inch (61-to-91-cm) lizard's speed has been timed at 21.7 mph (35 kmh).

Snakes with legs???

Scientists have found evidence that prehistoric snakes were creatures with tiny legs. Near Jerusalem, in 1978, geologist George Haas found a 97-million-year-old fossil of a creature with two stubby rear legs. He called it a lizard. Recently, scientists reexamined the bones, and they now believe it's the missing link between the snake and the lizard. This finding challenges the theory that snakes evolved solely from burrowing lizards, since the fossil represents a sea creature.

Ireland, A.D. 432

Famous (faulty) folktale: According to legend, St. Patrick drove the snakes out of Ireland. Stories are told of him standing on a hill, using a wooden staff to run the serpents into the sea. Possibly, this is a symbolic story, with the snakes representing old, pagan religions. In bringing Christianity to Ireland, St. Patrick effectively removed the old ways.

On a strictly scientific level, Ireland never had any snakes to begin with. About 15,000 years ago, Ireland was under a sheet of ice. As the ice melted, the sea level rose. The ocean separated Ireland from Britain before Ireland had a climate warm enough for snakes.

Speedy, Slinky Snakes

The black mamba wins the prize for fastest snake. It can move at speeds of 10 to 12 mph (16–19 kmh). The world's longest snake: a reticulated python that was measured at 32 feet 9.5 inches (9.9 m) long.

Activity

BAD RAP **Snakes in general have a bad reputation. Think about what snake features make people uncomfortable and write them down. What popular expressions and terms come from our negative feelings about snakes? "Venomous" is one example. Can you think of some famous bad snakes from literature and mythology? What are some arguments you could put forward to challenge popular notions that snakes are bad? Set up a debate in your class, with half of the class "pro-snake" and the other half "anti-snake."**

Checking Out Crocs

What does a crocodile's skin feel like? Is it cold to the touch? How much can a crocodile eat? Dr. Alison Leslie can tell you. She has spent the last several years studying the Nile crocodile in South Africa's St. Lucia Estuary. She hopes her research will help make sure that these endangered reptiles survive.

Lucky for Dr. Leslie and her fellow researchers, crocs prefer fish to humans. They also hunt other animals that live near the lake, such as zebras, porcupines, wildebeests, and even hippos. A full-grown croc, measuring as long as 16 feet (5 m) and weighing half a ton (453 kg), can charge out of the water at 40 miles (64 km) an hour, seize its prey, and carry it back within seconds.

The crocs at Lake St. Lucia didn't always appreciate being bothered by the researchers. Dr. Leslie admits that there have been a few close calls. "They have large teeth, powerful jaws," she says. "If you happen to be in the wrong place at the wrong time, crocodiles will take you." She's been bitten a few times by small crocodiles less than five feet (1.5 m) long. And one time, a huge male croc attacked the aluminum research boat. Luckily, the boat's driver spun the craft around and whisked it quickly away from the croc's territory.

Leslie's team is especially interested in studying crocodile nests and eggs. In South Africa, crocs mate in May or June, and the females lay their eggs in September and October. Unlike many other reptiles, female crocodiles watch their nests until the eggs hatch, and they protect their young after they're born. A female may lay anywhere between 25 and 100 eggs, which she keeps in a nest built from dead grass and plant matter covered with mud. In order for the eggs to develop, they must be kept between 80 and 94° F (27 and 34.5° C).

Like other reptiles, the temperature of the nest determines how many males or females will hatch. Dr. Leslie has studied this pattern in the Nile crocodile and made an interesting observation. "Turns out that temperatures below 31.7 degrees Celsius produce females," she explains. "Any temperature above that ... up until 34.5 degrees Celsius produces males."

Usually, when they saw the researchers approach, the mother crocodiles would leave their nests for the safety of the lake. The team quickly got out of the way whenever they saw a mother return unexpectedly.

Capturing Crocs

One way to protect the Nile crocodile is to make sure that its food supply isn't polluted, so Dr. Leslie carefully studies what the St. Lucia crocodiles eat. Generally, crocodiles can go long periods without food. In fact, a Nile crocodile probably only has about 50 big meals a year. The best way to learn about their diet is to capture them and look at what's inside their stomachs.

Capturing the crocodiles was no easy task. Often Dr. Leslie's team would work at night, shining spotlights on the water and looking out for those red crocodile eyes. A croc's eyes are set at the top of its head, close together. This gives the croc binocular vision, allowing it to spot its prey and judge how far away it is. Once the researchers saw a croc, they would throw a rope noose around its neck and haul the animal aboard their boat.

Larger crocs were caught on land with the help of a specially designed, baited trap at the lake

shore. The crocodile goes after the bait, passing through a rope noose. Triggered by the croc's movements, the noose snaps tight between its front and back legs.

No crocodile is going to let itself be poked and prodded without a fight, so the researchers used medicines to put the animal to sleep. Then, they slipped a special tool into its mouth and down into its stomach. This way, they were able to scoop out samples for testing. They had to be extra careful that they didn't damage the palatal valve at the rear of the croc's mouth; this valve closes off the croc's windpipe so it can use its jaws to catch prey underwater.

Rescuing These Reptiles

Crocodiles are endangered mainly because they have lost so much of their habitat. People have cleared wetlands and built houses on lake shores where crocodiles once built nests. Hunters have also killed many crocodiles for body parts, such as legs, tails, teeth, and skulls. Zulu hunters kill crocodiles for their bodily fluids, Leslie says. "The stomach acid and the fluid from the brain is incredibly acidic. It's sold to the witch doctor, who can use it as a potent poison." This may bring the hunter only a few dollars, but as long as crocodiles are seen as a source of money, they are at risk.

The more we understand about crocodiles, the better able we are to save them from extinction. Dr. Leslie and her colleagues are determined to collect as much information about the Nile crocodile as they can to help them survive.

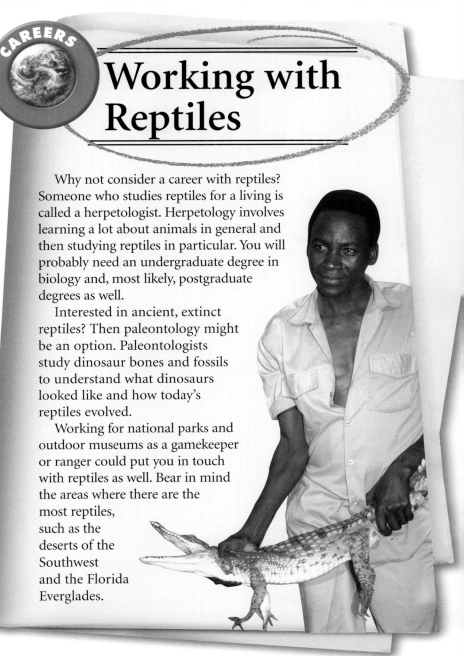

CAREERS

Working with Reptiles

Why not consider a career with reptiles? Someone who studies reptiles for a living is called a herpetologist. Herpetology involves learning a lot about animals in general and then studying reptiles in particular. You will probably need an undergraduate degree in biology and, most likely, postgraduate degrees as well.

Interested in ancient, extinct reptiles? Then paleontology might be an option. Paleontologists study dinosaur bones and fossils to understand what dinosaurs looked like and how today's reptiles evolved.

Working for national parks and outdoor museums as a gamekeeper or ranger could put you in touch with reptiles as well. Bear in mind the areas where there are the most reptiles, such as the deserts of the Southwest and the Florida Everglades.

Activity

SAVE THE CROCS! **Another endangered animal is the American crocodile, which lives in southern Florida. There may be only 500 left. Their population has been threatened by the construction of highways and waterfront homes and also mobile home parks. Poachers have also taken their toll.**

Find out what's being done in the Florida Everglades National Park to save the American crocodile. What would you do? What can residents do? How about the state government? Put together a proposal with recommendations for the private homeowner, the local business, the tourist, and the state legislature.

WHAT'S WRONG WITH THIS PICTURE?

Alaska, late August, 1999

You are camping out in the Alaskan tundra, enjoying the wide open, treeless views and the herds of caribou off in the distance. You go for a stroll, wading through the swamps created by the thawing ice and snow that cover this region for most of the year.

To your great surprise, you come across a log in the swamp. Knowing there are no trees anywhere nearby, you bend down for a closer look. Sure enough, it's no log but an alligator. It swims sluggishly away from you and comes to a stop just a few yards away. You look around and spot a mound made of mud and dead grasses—probably the alligator's nest. You are surprised to note that the mother alligator stays where she is, even though you take a few steps towards her nest.

A little further on, you meet a man on the trail who appears to be a scientist or naturalist. He looks the part, anyway, with his binoculars, notebooks, and sensible outdoor gear. You mention the alligator, and he nods knowingly. He explains that he's leading a conservation initiative to save the alligator by relocating some of these reptiles to Alaska. The waterlogged environment of the tundra, he explains, is the perfect solution. Every year the alligator's natural habitat in the American South gets smaller as people drain the swamps and clear the woods to build more houses. Undeveloped land in the tundra, on the other hand, is abundant, so he's brought some alligators up here for the summer months to see how they will breed.

As you listen, you realize this guy is no scientist but a complete crackpot. You are deeply disturbed by what you saw, and you immediately conclude that this relocation is going to be a complete disaster. List the factors that led to this conclusion and explain your reasoning.

Answers on page 32

28

clues

Use these clues ...

Alaskan tundra: fast facts

- **Short summer:** only 8 weeks in July and August

- **Average summer temperature:** 55° F (13° C) day; 32–40° F (0–4° C) night

- **Ground:** frozen much of the year; top layer thaws in summer, producing shallow lakes and swamps

- **Rainfall:** 12–20 inches (30–50 cm) per year

- **Wildlife:** waterfowl; birds of prey; mammals (lemmings, muskrats, bears, caribou); fish

OFF THE SCALES

Betcha Didn't Know That ...

- Crocodiles eat rocks. Eating rocks may help their digestion or add weight to help them stay underwater. About 20 percent of a crocodile's weight might be rocks.

- A venomous snake's forked tongue can't sting, although its saliva can be slightly toxic.

- It only takes 2 drops of venom from the black mamba snake to kill a human being.

- You can't tell a rattlesnake's age by the number of rattles it has. It gets a new one each time it sheds its skin, which could be five times a year. Also, old rattles can break off.

- Crocodiles have the biggest brains of any reptiles. Their brains are about the size of cigars.

- Crocodiles grow all their lives.

- The name *alligator* comes from the Spanish word *largato*, meaning "lizard."

- Chameleons hunt for insects by suddenly shooting out their very long tongues, which have sticky mucus at the end to trap the insect.

- Gecko eggs can stick to wood and survive out at sea. As a result, there are geckos on some islands where other lizards haven't yet arrived.

- Tuataras take 20 years to fully mature. They carry fertilized eggs for a full year before laying them, and then the eggs hatch 15 months later.

Reptile-ingo

Common words and expressions from the reptile world:

Turtleneck: a sweater or shirt with a long, stretchable neck, so called because it reminds us of the turtle's long neck when it peers its head out of its shell.

Crocodile tears: tears that are not from real sadness or pain; crocodiles have to get rid of extra salt in their systems through tear ducts in their eyes, but they are not "crying."

Serpentine: twisty and turny, like some roads.

Brain Teasers

What are we?
Many people think we are amphibians, but we're reptiles. Though many of us are exclusively aquatic, we all have characteristics of reptiles, including fully developed lungs. Our soft-shelled variety get oxygen from water through skin over their shells.

What am I?
People think I attack when unprovoked, but I only attack when I feel threatened. Of course, people may just be nervous around me because I can spit or spray venom at them from about 8 feet (2.4 m) away. My venom can blind them if I shoot it in their eyes.

(Answers on page 32)

Reptiles in literature

Long ago, before there were TVs, people used to entertain themselves with tales of natural phenomena. They used myths to explain aspects of their surroundings that they didn't understand scientifically. Reptiles appear often in mythology and folklore, frequently as mysterious, dangerous creatures.

Two of the most famous examples come from Greek mythology. Medusa was a wild woman who had snakes for hair. People were afraid of her because anyone caught looking into her eyes would turn to stone. She was finally killed by the Greek hero Perseus, who cut off her head. The winged horse, Pegasus, rose from her blood. The evil Cerberus also had a snake connection. He was a three-headed dog with a snake tail and snakes wrapped around his neck. Cerberus guarded the entrance to the underworld, Hades. One of Hercules's 12 labors was to conquer Cerberus.

Legends also arose of imaginary reptiles such as the dragon. Although no one had ever seen a dragon, storytellers passed on exciting tales of these fire-breathing, scaly creatures from faraway lands. Back then, there was a great deal of land that was unexplored, a thought that made people uncomfortable. They wondered what kinds of wild, dangerous creatures lurked beyond the familiar parts of the world. Sometimes people imagined the worst. Dragons also played an important role in legends about heroes such as Siegfried and Saint George. Anyone able to kill an enormous, fire-breathing monster many times his size was a hero, indeed.

Common misconceptions

Reptiles have always been mysterious creatures. Maybe that's why there are so many tall tales about their origins and features. Though many movies, cartoons, and books show people interacting with dinosaurs, the fact is that would have been impossible. Humans weren't around until about 65 million years after the dinosaurs became extinct! It's also wrong to think all those early reptiles were huge. Most dinosaurs were small or medium-sized. In fact, one of the smallest, *Compsognathus*, was only about 2 feet long and weighed 8 or 9 pounds.

Many people seem to believe that cobras love music and a snake charmers' horn can make them dance. Actually, like all snakes, cobras are deaf! They respond to the charmers' visual clues. It's all in the way he moves his horn.

And lizards' reputations have suffered. Some people think their bite is poisonous. In fact, few lizards give painful bites, and only two species are poisonous.

YOUR WORLD YOUR TURN

Final Project:
It's A Girl!

For many reptiles, particularly turtles, alligators, and crocodiles, the temperature of the nest determines the gender of the babies. If the nest is cool, more females will hatch. Warmer nests cause the eggs to hatch as males.

Sometimes hurricanes hit areas where sea turtles breed and nest. When this happens, scientists have to construct artificial shelters for the turtles to build nests and lay eggs in safety. The researchers must keep in mind the temperature variations when locating and building these shelters.

What sort of factors should the scientists consider? You can explore how temperatures are affected, as a way to determine whether a turtle egg will hatch as a male or a female.

Imagine you are living on an island in the Caribbean. A hurricane is approaching, and you and your classmates must quickly build several nesting shelters for the breeding sea turtles on your island. The first step is to find the best location.

You'll need:
- 3 outdoor thermometers
- graph paper
- colored pencils

① Find three dry areas on the ground near your classroom or home. One area should receive sunshine all day; one should receive sunshine only part of the day; and the third area should be in the shade all day long.

② Place a thermometer on the surface of each area. Record the temperature. Jot down other factors that might affect the temperature, such as whether there are clouds, rain, or wind.

③ Take thermometer readings every 30 minutes for one day. Record the information on a sheet of paper.

④ When you have completed your data, figure out the high, low, and average temperature for each area.

⑤ Use the graph paper and make a line graph. The temperature should be the vertical axis, and the half-hour segments should be on the horizontal axis. Plot the temperature variations for each nesting area using a different color pencil for each.

After completing your graph, discuss these questions with your classmates or family members:

- Which area had the highest average temperature? Which had the lowest? What factors in the environment affected the temperature in each place?

- Which would be the best area for producing more male baby turtles? Which would produce more females? Explain your answer based on the data collected.

- How would the temperatures be affected if the areas were kept moist? Discuss how you would find this out.

- Discuss how having too many males or too many females might upset the balance of nature where the turtles live and breed.

ANSWERS

Solve-It-Yourself Mystery, pages 28–29: The most disturbing thing you saw was the alligator's behavior: she moved sluggishly away when she saw you and didn't come forward when you approached her nest. Most female alligators will vigorously defend their nests from intruders, but because this one was surrounded by cold water, she was conserving energy. Her instincts and reactions were dulled as a result. Because the ground of the tundra is frozen much of the year, and the water just above freezing, the "naturalist" is crazy to think alligators could survive in this environment. Here it is, late August; fall coming right up. When winter arrives, the ground will be covered in ice and snow, the small mammals will be in hibernation until spring, the waterbirds will have migrated south, and the days will be short. Not only will the alligator lose much of its food supply, but its habitat will change radically. Without much sunlight, the alligator will be unable to get warm enough to survive. Worst of all, the eggs, which require temperatures ranging from 82–93° F (28–34° C), probably will not hatch.

Brain Teasers, page 30: *What are we?* Turtles and tortoises; *What am I?* Cobra